Changing How You Speak To Overcome Your Fear Of Speaking

Change techniques that will transform a speech into a memorable event

"Practical, proven techniques that will help you to make your next speech a success"

Dr. Jim Anderson

Published by:
Blue Elephant Consulting
Tampa, Florida

Copyright © 2014 by Dr. Jim Anderson

All rights reserved. No part of this book may be reproduced of transmitted in any form or by any means, electronic or mechanical, including photocopying, recording or by any information storage and retrieval system without written permission of the publisher, except for inclusion of brief quotations in a review.

Printed in the United States of America

Library of Congress Control Number: 2016919375

ISBN-13: 978-1540465641
ISBN-10: 1540465640

Warning – Disclaimer

The purpose of this book is to educate and entertain. This book does not promise or guarantee that anyone following the ideas, tips, suggestions, techniques or strategies will be hired. It is the discretion of employers if you will or will not be hired. The author, publisher and distributor(s) shall have neither liability nor responsibility to anyone with respect to any loss or damage caused, or alleged to be caused, directly or indirectly by the information contained in this book.

Recent Books By The Author

Product Management

- How Product Managers Can Sell More Of Their Product: Tips & Techniques For Product Managers To Better Understand How To Sell Their Product

- Product Development Lessons For Product Managers: How Product Managers Can Create Successful Products

Public Speaking

- Delivering Excellence: How To Give Presentations That Make A Difference: Presentation techniques that will transform a speech into a memorable event

- How To Rehearse In Order To Give The Perfect Speech: How to effectively rehearse your next speech to that your message be remembered forever!

CIO Skills

- What CIOs Need To Know In Order To Successfully Manage An IT Department: Decision Making Skills That Every CIO Needs To Have In Order To Be Able To Make The Right Choices

- How CIOs Can Make Innovation Happen: Tips And Techniques For CIOs To Use In Order To Make Innovation Happen In Their

IT Department

IT Manager Skills

- Building The Perfect Team: What Staffing Skills Do IT Managers Need?: Tips And Techniques That IT Managers Can Use In Order To Correctly Staff Their Teams

- Secrets Of Effective Leadership For IT Managers: Tips And Techniques That IT Managers Can Use In Order To Develop Leadership Skills

Negotiating

- Use The Power Of Arguing To Win Your Next Negotiation: How To Develop The Skill Of Effective Arguing In A Negotiation In Order To Get The Best Possible Outcome

- Learn How To Signal In Your Next Negotiation: How To Develop The Skill Of Effective Signaling In A Negotiation In Order To Get The Best Possible Outcome

Miscellaneous

- How To Heal A Broken Leg – Fast!: Understanding how to deal with a broken leg in order to start walking again quickly

- How Software Defined Networking (SDN) Is Going To Change Your World Forever: The Revolution In Network Design And How It Affects

Note: See a complete list of books by Dr. Jim Anderson at the back of this book.

Acknowledgements

Any book like this one is the result of years of real-world work experience. In my over 25 years of working for 7 different firms, I have met countless fantastic people and I've been mentored by some truly exceptional ones. Although I've probably forgotten some of the people who made me the person that I am today, here is my attempt to finally give them the recognition that they so truly deserve:

- Thomas P. Anderson
- Art Puett
- Bobbi Marshall
- Bob Boggs

Dr. Jim Anderson

This book is dedicated to my family: Lori, Maddie, Nick, and Ben. None of this would have been possible without their constant love and support.

Thanks for always believing in me and providing me with the strength to always be willing to go out there and be my best for you.

Table Of Contents

OVERCOMING YOUR FEAR OF SPEAKING 8

ABOUT THE AUTHOR 10

CHAPTER 1: HOW SPEAKERS HANDLE THAT FEAR THING... 15

CHAPTER 2: BOO! HOW SPEAKERS OVERCOME THEIR FEAR OF SPEAKING 20

CHAPTER 3: REAL LIFE SPEAKING LESSONS: LEARNING FROM A KEYNOTE 24

CHAPTER 4: PUBLIC SPEAKER CHALLENGES: ATTACK OF THE NERVES! 28

CHAPTER 5: REMEMBER WHAT HAPPENS WHEN A SPEAKER STOPS GROWING... 32

CHAPTER 6: GREAT SPEAKERS AREN'T AFRAID TO STUMBLE ON THE WAY TO THE TOP 36

CHAPTER 7: A PUBLIC SPEAKER'S PLAN TO FIGHT STAGE FRIGHT 40

CHAPTER 8: WHAT CAN MAKE A PUBLIC SPEAKER NERVOUS? 44

CHAPTER 9: TOO SHY, SHY – HOW TO OVERCOME YOUR SHYNESS AND BECOME A PUBLIC SPEAKER 48

CHAPTER 10: HOW GOOD OF A SPEAKER YOU ARE DEPENDS ON HOW WELL YOU SEE YOURSELF 52

CHAPTER 11: NEW TECHNIQUES FOR DEALING WITH EVERY SPEAKER'S BIGGEST FEAR: STAGE FRIGHT 57

CHAPTER 12: YOUR SPEECH IS NOT OVER WHEN YOU ARE DONE TALKING 61

Overcoming Your Fear Of Speaking

Standing up in front of a group of people and giving a speech is not an easy thing to do for any of us. As we stand there with everyone's eyes on us, it can be very easy to become overwhelmed with nerves and fear. However, if we are going to be successful public speakers, then we need to learn to deal with our fears.

Fear and public speaking seem to go hand in hand. As we prepare to take the stage, it's all too common that we'll suddenly get an attack of the nerves. We fear that once we start our speech, we're going to make a mistake or say something wrong. Stage fright can take over.

What we need to understand is that the people who are really good public speakers were once in our position. However, they moved forward. No, they were not always perfect – they stumbled just like we do. However, they learned from their mistakes and they become better over time. No matter what causes you to become afraid or shy, you can identify it and then you can overcome it.

In order to master our fears, we need to be able to take a step back. We need to look at ourselves and understand how our audience is viewing us. It's only by doing this that we'll be able to become a better speaker.

We also have to remember that if we can master our fears and actually deliver a great speech, our job is not over when we are done speaking. In fact, our interaction with our audience may just be beginning at this point in time.

For more information on what it takes to be a great public speaker, check out my blog, The Accidental Communicator, at:

www.TheAccidentalCommunicator.com

Good luck!

- Dr. Jim Anderson

About The Author

I must confess that I never set out to be a public speaker. When I went to school, I studied Computer Science and thought that I'd get a nice job programming and that would be that. Well, at least part of that plan worked out!

My first job was working for Boeing on their F/A-18 fighter jet program. I spent my days programming fighter jet software in assembly language and I loved it. The U.S. government decided to save some money and went looking for other countries to sell this plane to. This put me into an unfamiliar role: I started to meet with foreign military officials and I ended up having to give speeches in order to explain what my product did.

Time moved on and so did I. I found myself working for Siemens, the big German telecommunications company. They were making phone switches and selling them to the seven U.S. phone companies. The problem was that the switches were too complicated. Customers couldn't tell the difference between one complicated phone switch from another complicated phone switch. Once again I found myself standing in front of the room giving speeches in order to explain what these complicated machines did and why ours were better than anyone else's.

I've spent over 25 years working as a product manager for both big companies and startups. This has given me an opportunity to do many, many presentations for customers, at conferences, and everywhere in-between.

I now live in Tampa Florida where I spend my time managing my consulting business, Blue Elephant Consulting, teaching college courses at the University of South Florida, and traveling to work with companies like yours to share the knowledge that I have about how to create and deliver powerful and effective speeches.

I'm always available to answer questions and I can be reached at:

Dr. Jim Anderson
Blue Elephant Consulting
Email: jim@BlueElephantConsulting.com
Facebook: http://goo.gl/1TVoK
Web: **www.BlueElephantConsulting.com**

"Unforgettable communication skills that will set your ideas free…"

Create Speeches That Motivate Your Audiences And Get Your Message Heard!

Dr. Jim Anderson is available to provide training and coaching on the topics that are the most important to people who have to speak in public: how can I create a speech that people want to hear and how can I deliver in a way that will allow me to connect with my audience and get my point across to them?

Dr. Anderson believes that in order to both learn and remember what he says, speakers need to laugh. Each one of his speeches is full of fun and humor so that what he says "sticks" with everyone.

Dr. Anderson's Public Speaking Training Includes:

1. How to plan your next speech: pick your purpose and understand your audience.
2. What's the best way to get PowerPoint and Keynote to work with you, not against you?
3. What do you need to do when you are presenting in order to truly connect with your audience?

Dr. Jim Anderson presents over 100 speeches per year. To invite Dr. Anderson to speak at your event, contact him at:

Phone: 813-418-6970 or
Email: jim@BlueElephantConsulting.com

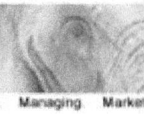

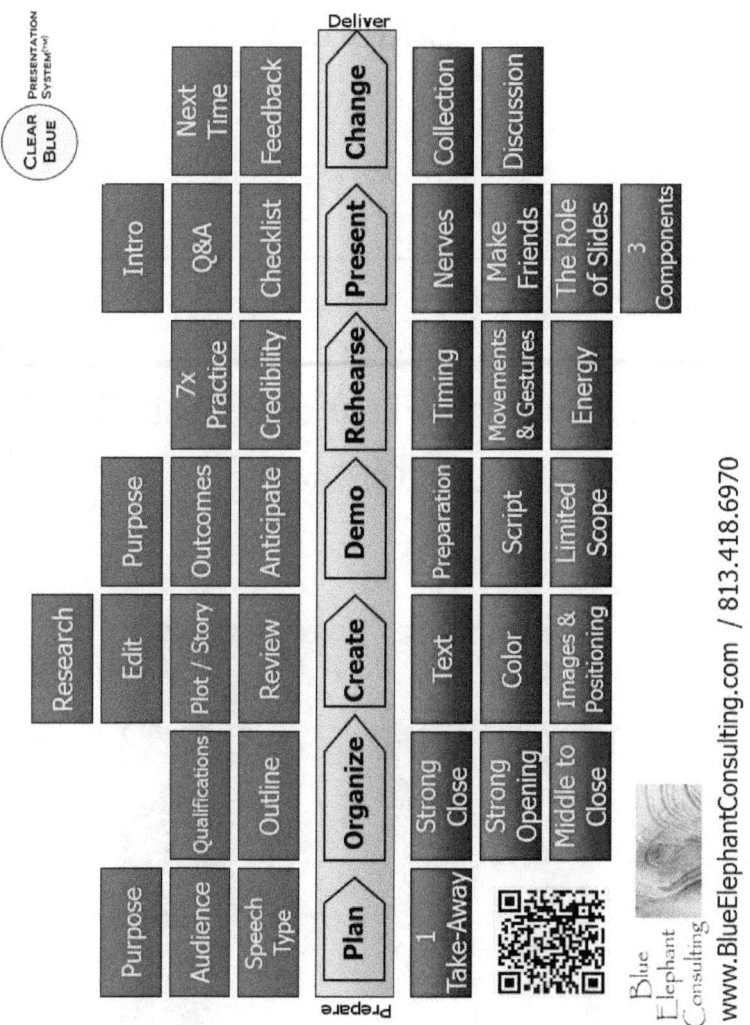

Blue Elephant Consulting has created the **Clear Blue™ Presentation System** for creating and delivering powerful and memorable presentations. The contents of this book are based on lessons learned during the development of the Clear Blue system. Contact Blue Elephant Consulting to learn more about the Clear Blue presentation system.

Chapter 1

How Speakers Handle That FEAR Thing...

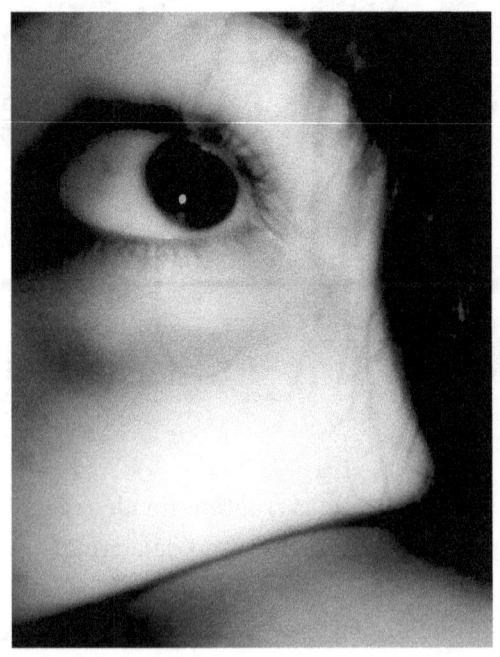

Chapter 1: How Speakers Handle That FEAR Thing...

Remember when your Mom was tucking you into your bed at night and she told you that there was nothing to be afraid of so that you could go to sleep? Well guess what, she was only partially right. It turns out that a whole lot of us have a deep down fear of getting up in front a bunch of people and opening our mouth. Let's see if we can do something about this...

So What Are We Really Afraid Of?

Before we go running off and trying to solve a problem that doesn't really exist, let's first do some checking and make sure that we have a real problem here. Over at The New Book of Lists: The Original Compendium of Curious Information they've got a list (what else?) of what scares us the most:

1. Speaking before a group
2. Heights
3. Insects and bugs
4. Financial problems
5. Deep water
6. Sickness
7. Death
8. Flying
9. Loneliness
10. Dogs

So there you go, we seem to be more afraid of speaking in public than we are of going broke or dogs. Clearly we've got to do something about this issue.

Create Your Own Cruise Control

So let's all agree that if speaking in public is what scares us, then the first words out of our mouths while giving a speech are the ones that will be the hardest to do. Since we know that this is going to be difficult to do, we should probably come up with a way to make it easier to do.

This is where the idea of putting yourself on cruise control comes in. If you take the time to write out and memorize the first two minutes of your speech, then you won't have to worry about what you are going to say. By doing this we give ourselves two minutes to get our act together and allow the butterflies in our gut to line up in formation and fly straight.

Plan Your Introductions

Since the memorization of the first two minutes went so well, let's build on that. Your speech is going to be made up of a series of things: points, stories, questions, etc. Each of these components needs an introduction even if it's only a few words.

Take the time to memorize the exact words that you want to come out of your mouth when you are starting a new piece of your speech and this will serve to "anchor" you on that topic and, once again, you'll have an automatic sense of direction on what you want to say next.

Cheat Like There Is No Tomorrow

Remember in school when it came to be test time and your teachers had you put all of your papers away before you started the test? Well guess what, that was then and this is now. You are more than welcome to cheat as much as you'd like when you are giving a speech.

In order to do a good job of cheating, you're going to need a cheat sheet. The cheat sheet needs to be easy to read – that means use a nice big font and space everything out. Short of writing your speech out word-for-word, you're going to want to put on your cheat sheet whatever it's going to take to help you remember what you want to say.

Rehearse And Then Rehearse Some More

Do I even have to go over this one? If you are the type of person who gets a rush from just showing up and doing something without practicing it beforehand, then do us all a favor and don't speak in public.

If you are willing to do some rehearsing before you give a speech, then good for you. My clients are always asking me how many times they should practice a speech before giving it. My answer is always the same: 7 times. It turns out that this seems to be the magic number that sits at the dividing line between too few and too many practices.

Buy Yourself Some Time

When it comes to speaking in public, time is often our worst enemy. All too often you see speakers showing up just in time (or late) to give their speech. They run to the front of the room, all flustered, and then try to calm down and give a speech.

Instead of putting yourself in this position, plan on showing up to where you'll be speaking at least an hour before you are scheduled to go on stage. If you can get there even earlier, then that would be even better. This is almost like buying yourself an insurance policy that when it's time for you to speak, you'll be more than ready.

What All Of This Means For You

To feel fear when you think about standing in front of a group of people and speaking to them is very natural. However, it's one of the things in life that has to be done and so you need to find ways to overcome your fear.

Much of what you can do to conquer your fear can be done long before it comes time for you to speak. Memorizing parts of your speech, creating a cheat sheet, and making sure that you show up early will all help you to remain in control of your fears.

Realizing that everyone feels the same way about public speaking can go a long way in helping you to find the courage to do it. Now just put into practice some of these suggestions and not only will you be able to do it, but you'll be able to do it well...!

Chapter 2

Boo! How Speakers Overcome Their Fear Of Speaking

Chapter 2: Boo! How Speakers Overcome Their Fear Of Speaking

Considering just how much effort it takes to give a speech, it's perfectly natural that every speaker should feel at least some level of nervousness. However, when we start to "shut down" because we're so scared about giving a speech that's when we start to realize that this whole nervousness thing has gotten out of hand. What's a speaker to do?

Press The Flesh

There truly can be nothing more nerve-racking than standing in front of a group of strangers and trying to give a speech. Since you know that this is not what you want to do, you should find a way to change the game.

A simple and easy way to do this is to make sure that you have time to meet some or all of your audience before your speech starts. The process of meeting people, learning their names, shaking hands with them, and basically getting to know them can work miracles.

All of a sudden a room full of strangers who you may have believed didn't really care to hear what you are going to be talking about will have been transformed into a gathering of friends who are eager and interested in hearing what you have to say. Who would be afraid of talking to friends?

Remember To Breath

A most curious thing happens whenever we start to get nervous or afraid: we stop breathing. Hopefully it goes without saying that this is a bad thing when you are going to be giving a speech.

When you get nervous, you start to take a series of short, shallow breaths that don't give the stale air in your lungs a chance to clear out. This means that your body isn't getting enough oxygen and so very quickly you'll start to have a faster heart rate, difficulty breathing, etc.

Once again the cure is quite simple. When you realize that this is what you are doing, stop and take several deep breaths. This will provide your lungs with the air that they need and should help to make all of those symptoms of nervousness go away.

Pull Yourself Up

When we become nervous, we start to build up a lot of (what else?) nervous energy. If you don't want to appear to be nervous to your audience, then what you've got to do is to find a way to get rid of this nervous energy.

When you are sitting on a chair on stage waiting for the announcer to complete your introduction, your options for venting nervous energy are limited. However, don't despair, there's an old trick that the pros use that will help you out.

Simply place both of your hands on the sides of the bottom of the chair that you are sitting on and proceed to pull up for a few minutes. Unless you are Harry Potter, that chair isn't going anywhere with you sitting on it and you'll be discreetly venting some of that nervous energy. Relax and try it again to vent even more energy.

Let's Get Physical

This one takes a bit longer to do, but it also comes with long-term payoffs. Taking the time to get physically fit is a great way to keep your nerves under control.

By finding a physical exercise that you enjoy doing, you'll have come up with a way to vent that nervous energy long before you are standing on a stage. It doesn't matter if you take up running, walking, biking or whatever. Just as long as you keep moving, your nerves won't be able to keep up with you.

What All Of This Means For You

Being a speaker means being nervous. In one way this is a good thing: your nerves will keep you alert and full of energy. However, having too much nervous energy means that it will start to spill out and your audience will become distracted by just how nervous you are.

What you need to do is to find ways that work for you to keep your nervous energy under control. Meeting your audience, remembering to breathe properly, and exercising can all help you to do this.

In the end it's your words that you want your audience to remember about your speech, not how nervous you seemed to be. Follow these suggestions and you'll come across as a cool and confident speaker who really knows their stuff.

Chapter 3

Real Life Speaking Lessons: Learning From A Keynote

Chapter 3: Real Life Speaking Lessons: Learning From A Keynote

We can talk about how to give better speeches until we're blue in the face, but in the end **it's what we see** that will really change how we give speeches. With that thought in mind I'd like to share with you a critique of a keynote speech that I had a chance to see the other day. Listen and learn from the efforts of others...

What The Speaker Did Right

Anyone who gets picked to deliver a keynote has got to be **a good speaker**, right? This speaker was a good speaker and it showed in a number of the ways that he gave his speech.

His work experience came from the gas and oil exploration industry. What this meant is that he had a lot of **very good stories**. However, that's only the half of it – he was also a very good story teller. Throughout his speech he worked in personal stories that reinforced the point that he was making. Soon the audience was anticipating his next story.

His delivery style came across as being **strong and confidant**. His voice boomed out from the podium and there was no problem hearing him as he spoke. Clearly he had given this speech before and his delivery style was polished, not hesitant.

As he gave his speech, he looked at and spoke to the audience. He may have been using notes, but it sure didn't show. His eyes remained on the audience during the entire speech and every member of the audience was left with the feeling that the speaker had been **talking directly to him** during the entire time.

What The Speaker Did Wrong

No speech or speaker is ever perfect and, of course, this speaker was no exception. One of the biggest mistakes that he made was that he was unsure of **where to stand** during his speech.

The **stage setup** was a bit unusual for this speech. The podium was off to the left of the stage and the rest of the stage was taken up by a row of chairs that had tables in front of them – it was set for a panel discussion.

The speaker desperately **wanted to pace** while he was talking. This is exactly what he ended up doing. However, from the audience it was a bit odd to see the speaker walking back and forth behind a row of chairs and tables. What he should have done was to remain behind the podium so that we would not have been distracted.

What to do with your hands is always a question that every speaker has to deal with. This speaker did an effective job of using his hands to make gestures that supported what he was saying. However, when he wasn't making gestures he had the bad habit of **putting his hands into his pockets**. I was sitting off to the side and this was pretty distracting.

Finally, although the speech was good, **the ending seemed rushed**. We were traveling along at 60 miles-per-hour and then all of a sudden we pulled off to the side of the road and stopped — the speech was over. The speaker needed to have done a better job of winding the speech down and making his final points.

What This Means For You

As speakers, we would do well to **learn from the efforts of other speakers**. Every time we see someone else give a speech, we should watch them carefully and take good notes.

In the case of the keynote speaker that I had an opportunity to watch, he did a number of things very well. Chief among these were the **compelling stories** that he told – when he was doing this he was able to completely hold the audience's attention.

There were several areas that he could have improved on. The one that stood out the most was the fact that he **didn't know where to stand** while giving his speech – he ended up pacing back and forth behind chairs on the stage which was very distracting.

No speech is ever perfect. We'd all like to find ways to make our next speech be better than the one that we gave last time. One of the best ways to make this happen is to take the time to **truly watch other speakers** do their best to deliver a speech. By learning from others we can become better ourselves…

Chapter 4

Public Speaker Challenges: Attack Of The Nerves!

Chapter 4: Public Speaker Challenges: Attack Of The Nerves!

All that I'm asking for is **some simple rules** that would govern our lives. Among these rules would this little gem: I've got no problem having to deal with being nervous as a beginning speaker; however, once I've been speaking for a while I should no longer have any problems with nerves. Dang it – it turns out that these rules don't exist and speakers can have panic attacks at any time no matter how much experience they have...

Where Does The Panic Come From?

When you've never felt a sense of panic before (or if it's been a really, really long time since you felt it), then the first question that will pop into your mind when panic arrives is **"What's causing this?"** As with all such things in life, the answer is probably somewhat complicated.

If you don't normally have to deal with a case of the nerves when you are either preparing or actually giving a speech, then clearly something has changed. You need to take the time to search your environment in order to **identify what's different**.

There are a number of **common causes** that make experienced speakers nervous. Who's in your audience is one of them. More often than not, when you have someone that you know in the audience you can start to become jittery. This can include family members, friends, or even just people that you respect.

If you are having **your speech recorded** in some manner (either sound or video or both), then the need to be perfect can cause you problems. It's not that the recording is that big of a deal, it's just that it may be a different environment from what you are normally used to.

Finally, someone asked you to stand up and give a speech. **You want to do a good job for them**. The more important that your speech is for them and their career, the more pressure that there will be on you and the higher the probability that you'll experience some level of panic.

How To Deal With Nerves

Understanding why you are dealing with a sudden case of the nerves is **a good first start**. Now you need to find a way to make them go away. The good news here is that this is possible and it's really not all that hard to do.

Let's cover the basics first: **what not to do**. Skip the caffeine. No matter how you get your drug of choice whether it's from coffee or soda, just say no on the day that you'll be speaking. Skip the milk. Same thing goes for dairy products because they can leave a coating on your mouth and throat that you don't need to be dealing with. Finally, do I even have to tell you to stay away from alcohol (for obvious reasons)?

Since there is no way to tell what kind of shape your throat is going to be in before you give a speech and since becoming panicky can **cause your throat to dry out**, bring some throat lozenges along and pop them as needed. Couple this with some deep breathing exercises and you will be on your way to regaining control over your nerves.

Nerves have a lot to do with **nervous energy**. If you can cause this energy to go away, you'll have less energy to be nervous with. The quickest and easiest way to do this is to perform some stretching exercises. I'm not talking about jumping jacks here, but rather leg and arm extensions that will stretch you out.

Finally, you need to turn that **room full of strangers** into a room full of people that you know. The fastest way to do this is to take the time to meet as many people as possible before you get up and give your speech. Shaking their hand, introducing yourself, and finding out a little bit about them will win them over to your side before you even open your mouth.

What All Of This Means For You

No matter how comfortable you are standing in front of an audience, there is always the possibility that at some point in time you'll have to deal with **a case of the nerves**. The good news is that this can be a temporary situation.

When this happens, the first thing that you need to do is to take the time to **understand what is causing it**. Next, you need to focus on taking actions that will allow you to relieve the stress that you are feeling.

Sometimes the best realization is that panic attacks are **temporary things** – they won't last. As speakers we need to realize that we are providing a service for our audiences and this is why we go through the effort of creating and delivering speeches. Focus on this and all of your temporary fears will melt away…

Chapter 5

Remember What Happens When A Speaker Stops Growing...

Chapter 5: Remember What Happens When A Speaker Stops Growing…

As speakers, you'd hope that we'd always be looking for ways to boost our speaking skills. However, it turns out that all too often this is not the case. There can be many reasons, but the end result is the same: we reach a given level in our speaking and then **we just "hold" there**. Not getting any worse, but at the same time not getting any better. Let's take a look at what causes this and see how we can keep moving forward.

Why Do We Stall In Our Speaking Careers?

When we are first starting out as speakers, we understand that **we're not very good**. We realize this because we are very attuned to the feedback that we're getting from our audience – they are bored and restless when we are speaking.

Because we know that we're not very good, **we are open to change**. We don't want to have our audiences dread it when we approach the front of the room to give a talk. This means that we're open to listening to what other people say about our speaking style. We also keep our eyes open and watch other speakers so that we can learn from them.

All of these different inputs cause something magical to happen: **we become better speakers**. It doesn't happen overnight, but rather it happens little by little. All of a sudden we find that we're actually pretty good speakers: we don't fear standing in front of an audience and talking and the audience almost seems to be looking forward to listening to us talk.

However, this is when something bad can also start to happen: we plateau. Once we've reached this level of speaking, we can decide that we're **"good enough"** and we stop. We stop listening to what our audience is trying to tell us and we stop listening to how others evaluate our speaking.

That's why the world is filled with speakers who are **just adequate**. They've reached a level where they are "good enough" and then they stalled. If you can't detect that you are in a rut and if you are not motivated to get yourself out of it, then that's where you'll spend the rest of your speaking days.

How To Leave Your Comfort Zone And Become A Better Speaker

So no matter if you are **in a rut** currently or if you fear that you may be starting to enter a rut, spending the rest of your days there does not have to be your fate. It turns out that there are a number of different things that you can do in order to pull yourself out of this situation:

Change!: the biggest reason that we get stuck in ruts is because our speaking opportunities become too predictable. Change things up – offer to talk about a topic that you've not talked about before or change how you present the material that you've given over and over again. Different is good!

Ask For Opinions: what helped you to become a better speaker back in the early days was that you were open to the comments offered by others. Invite someone whose opinion you respect to attend your next speech and provide you with feedback. When they do, take action based on what they tell you.

Picture The Future: better than anyone else, you know what a better you as a speaker would look like. The first step in getting to there is to mentally picture yourself as that better speaker. Once you've done that, you can start to map out the steps that you need to take to get there.

Baby Steps: Becoming a better speaker is what we all want to do. In order to make this happen, we need to ease ourselves into the future taking things one step at a time. We didn't get to be the speakers that we are today overnight and it's going to take mastering a sequence of steps to get to where we want to be.

What All Of This Means For You

Getting stuck in a rut is an easy thing to do. As speakers, those ruts can hold us back from **becoming better speakers**. The first thing that we need to do is to realize when we've gotten stuck in a rut and why. The next is to find a way to get out of it.

Getting out of a speaker's rut is a tricky thing to do. The key is to **shake things up**: get used to change, get outside advice, and picture the future that you want.

Getting stuck in a rut can happen to any speaker. Getting out of that rut is the key to **becoming a successful speaker**. If you want to keep developing your speaking skills, then you need to do a "rut check" and then take action to get out if you are in one.

Chapter 6

Great Speakers Aren't Afraid To Stumble On The Way To The Top

Chapter 6: Great Speakers Aren't Afraid To Stumble On The Way To The Top

A quick question for you: **are you afraid to fail?** Would you be willing to get up and give a speech if you knew that it was going to turn out badly? Even though we all know the importance of public speaking, I'm willing to bet that a lot of us would say "no" – speakers who do a good job get asked to speak again, those who don't are never asked back. However, I'm going to tell you that you're wrong – get ready to fail if you want to succeed.

How To Kill Your Public Speaking Development

In your speaking opportunities right now, what would happen to you if you failed? That post event review would be a tough one to sit through, right? Let's face it, failure is not something that is rewarded in our speaking opportunities and in fact it's something that **we all actively avoid** if we possibly can. The benefits of public speaking are great, but failing at giving a speech is something that none of us wants to do.

However, maybe we're just setting ourselves up for a much bigger disaster. Can we all admit that **the world as we know it is changing**? What audiences are looking for in a speech is changing and in our world of iPhones, and Twitter we are now competing with many other sources of information all the time. We all know that the way that the world used to be is long gone.

Something else is changing also: what is asked for when you give a speech. The first speech that you ever gave probably wouldn't be asked for these days – things have moved along. The speech that you may be preparing to give, no matter how many clever presentation tips you are planning on using, probably won't asked for in what, 2, maybe 3 years from now. This all means that **you are going to have to change** and change involves risk and along with risk comes the very real possibility that you are going to fail.

How To Become A Success By Failing

Well, that failing stuff doesn't sound like it's going to be any fun. But wait, **has anyone else ever failed?** Turns out that yes, in fact most successful people can look at their past and point to failures that helped them to get to where they are now.

The poster child for this kind of "good failure" would be Howard Schultz – the guy who founded **the Starbucks chain of coffee shops**. We all know and love the Starbucks store today, but when Howard first started it he really blew it. There were no chairs, he played lots of opera music, and his menu was in Italian. Clearly he quickly realized that he had failed, adjusted, and went on to become a big success.

You can do the same. You just need to **learn to make lots of small bets** when you give a speech. Some of these bets will pay off, and some won't. It's through what you learn from the failures that you'll be able to make tiny changes to your approach and try, try again.

If we keep doing things the same way that we've always been doing them, then we will eventually stagnate and then **we'll go into decline**. However, if you have the courage to start to fail and to learn from those failures, then the future contains limitless possibilities for both you and your speeches.

What All Of This Means For You

Speakers who are afraid to fail **will never become a true success**. Oh sure, they may do ok for a few years, but when things get really rough, they'll wash out.

If you are willing to adjust how you view failure, **your speaking can take off**. If you can start to look at failures as simply being learning experiences that are not be feared, but are to be used to become a better speaker then you'll be able to grow and become better at what you do.

No, you can't be an idiot about this and do silly things that cause your speech to fail – don't try to test your audience's listening skills, but if you try your hardest and your speech still fails than **you will have learned what doesn't work**. The big deal is that it takes courage for you to be able to do this.

Speakers who are a success have to had failures in their past. It's from the forge of failure that the steel of success is formed. Learn how to make small bets so that **you can learn what works** and what doesn't. Do this well and you'll become a successful public spea

ker.

Chapter 7

A Public Speaker's Plan To Fight Stage Fright

Chapter 7: A Public Speaker's Plan To Fight Stage Fright

It's **you vs. stage fright**. Who's going to win the next time that you are asked to give a speech? It turns out that this is one battle that you can always emerge a victor from. However, in order to make this happen you are going to have to prepare yourself for battle before the speech starts...

Don't Do The Wrong Thing Before You Speak

When you are getting ready to give a speech, forget using any clever presentation tips, your stage fright may show up and want to do battle. If this happens, you need to **know what not to do** just as much as you need to know what you should be doing.

Although we all know what the importance of public speaking is, we can be stopped in our tracks by a serious case of stage fright. Each one of us reacts to the challenge of dealing with stage fright in a different way. However, it comes across in the same way – **our body exhibits some sort of reaction**. This is going to be the key to not doing the wrong things.

All too often we have received some sort of suggestion in the past from somebody as to **how we should prepare to battle our stage fright**. More often than not, these suggestions have something to do with how we should prepare our body in order to give our speech even with stage fright standing there before us.

What many speakers do in order to take on their stage fright is to **make some sort of physical movement before they start to speak**. This can be a simple as either tensing or stretching your body. The reason that we do this is because we are trying to "puff" ourselves up.

There are a lot of different names for this kind of posturing. At different times we call it "standing tall" or even "anchoring". No matter what you end up calling it, **it's the wrong thing to do**. The reason that this is such a bad idea is because of what it does to our voices. We end up tensing up the muscles that we use for breathing – and that makes it even harder to breath. Tensing your body will result in sore muscles half way through your speech. All of these factors will result in you being distracted while you are speaking and will take away from your message.

What To Do Before You Speak To Make Sure That You Win The Battle

Now that you know what you shouldn't do before your next speech when you have to do battle with your stage fright, the big question is **just exactly what should you be doing?**

The first thing to do is to **find out what you are doing wrong** – because we all do different things. So, pretend for just a moment that you are standing off to the right of the stage that in a few moments you will be occupying in order to deliver a speech. What I'm going to want you to do is to stand up and walk onto that pretend stage.

While you are doing this, **observe what you are doing with your body**. Are you tightening your upper body or are you starting to do some stretching in order to prepare yourself to take the stage? If you are doing either one of these things, then this is exactly what you need to stop doing before your next speech.

Instead, what you are going to want to be doing is to **work at getting comfortable with being yourself**. Ultimately, the real you is what your audience wants to see and what they'll use their listening skills to hear because that is what they are going to be able to connect with. A puffed up version of you is going to seem to be strange and unusual to them and they won't want to connect with you when you are like that.

If you find yourself struggling to be your true self, then a great way to calm down and allow this to happen is to **get more physical exercise before you take the stage**. It can be as simple as taking a walk around the building or going up and down a set of stairs a few times. Use these exercises to work off some of your nervous energy and you'll be able to settle into who you really are – you!

What All Of This Means For You

When faced with a case of stage fight, we all have the same decision to make: **stand our ground or run away**. If you choose to do battle with your stage fright because you know what the benefits of public speaking are, then you are going to have to go into battle prepared to win.

In order to ensure that you will emerge from this fight as the victor, **you are going to have to do a couple of things**. The first is that you are going to have to stop doing the pre-speech physical activities that you think that are helping you but which are really harming your ability to deliver a good speech. Next, you are going to have to start to do the things that will prepare you both physically and mentally to focus on your speech and not on your stage fright.

Stage fright is a fear that can be defeated. The trick to accomplishing this task is to win the fight before your speech starts. Follow these rules and you'll stop doing the things that you shouldn't be doing and you'll start doing the things that you should be doing. That's the way that you win a fight even before it starts!

Chapter 8

What Can Make A Public Speaker Nervous?

Chapter 8: What Can Make A Public Speaker Nervous?

As speakers we all know that just before we get ready to stand before an audience we can become very nervous. This just seems to be a part of life despite the importance of public speaking. However, here's the big question – **why do we become so nervous all of the time** and what can we do about it?

Becoming Nervous Because Of The Situation

The #1 reason that you and I may become nervous before our next speech is simply because we fear standing before and talking **to this particular audience in this room right now**. There can be a whole bunch of reasons why: it's a big audience, we've never been in this place before, etc.

When this happens, we need transform the speaking event into an event that won't make us nervous. Generally, when we're talking with friends we are not nervous. That's why you need to **mentally recast the speech that you are just about to give** in this strange place to a speech that you would have with a group of close friends in a more comfortable setting.

Becoming Nervous Because Of The Audience

Another reason that we may become nervous before we give a speech is because **we don't know the audience that we'll be talking to**. Are these important people? Are these people who may know more about your topic than you do?

There's no simple way to tackle this challenge. However, if you sit down before the speech and think it through you can make yourself less nervous. **Picture yourself delivering a great**

speech, your audience enjoying what you are saying, and you receiving a standing ovation when you are done. Simply by mentally "seeing" all of this happen, you'll feel yourself becoming more calm when it comes time to deliver the speech because you'll feel that you've already done it once before.

Becoming Nervous Because Of Your Goal

Every speech that we give is done for a reason. **We always have some goal that we are trying to accomplish** – there is something that we want. The more that we think about how important achieving this goal is, the more nervous we may become if we start to spend too much time thinking about what will happen if we are not able to convince our audience to support our goal.

The trick to becoming less nervous about your goal is to **find ways to focus on the here and now and not the future**. It's really what's going to happen in the future that is going to make you nervous. This means that you are going to want to focus on what's going on in your speech right now and that will push thoughts of the future off to the side and thus reduce your nervousness.

What All Of This Means For You

I've got some bad news about being nervous for you – **it's just a normal part of life**. As speakers we always seem to become nervous before we get ready to give a speech. What we want to do is to find ways to deal with this feeling so that we can share the benefits of public speaking with our audience.

It turns out that there are **three different reasons** that we become nervous before a speech: the situation, the audience, and the goals that we want to accomplish. Each of these sources of nervousness can be dealt with in order to decrease their impact.

We will never be able to **not be nervous before a speech** – we are human after all. However, if you follow the tips that we've covered then the next time that you give a speech you should be just a little bit less nervous!

Chapter 9

Too Shy, Shy – How To Overcome Your Shyness An Become A Public Speaker

Chapter 9: Too Shy, Shy – How To Overcome Your Shyness And Become A Public Speaker

When we take a look at all of the things that can hold us back from becoming the great speaker that we want to be, what always seems to be at the top of the list? More often than not, **it's a fear of public speaking**. There can be many reasons for this fear, but one of the main culprits is always a bad case of shyness. Here's what you can do to overcome this.

Start To Overcome Your Shyness Slowly

If, despite knowing the importance of public speaking, you are dealing with shyness, then there's nothing that you are going to be able to do that is going to make it go away overnight. Instead, you are going to have to **come up with a plan** that will allow you to slowly overcome your shyness.

A great way to start this process is to sit down and take the time to **identify something that you feel that you do very well**. We all have some skill that we're just a little bit better at than most people. Identify this skill and then work at it – become even better at doing what you do well. Knowing that you have a skill that you are good at will fill you with confidence and when you work this skill, or a discussion of it, into your next speech you'll have started to overcome your shyness.

A lot of our shyness comes from **a fear of interacting with people that we don't know**. This is something that you're going to have to work up to overcoming. A great way to start this process is to practice speaking to close friends and family members. Once you can do this easily, start to widen the circle of people that you talk to in order to include friends that you are not so close to. Keep widening your circle and eventually add strangers. This all takes a while to do, but you'll be amazed with how easy it eventually becomes to talk to a room full of people that you don't know.

In order to overcome your shyness, you are going to have to **want to overcome it**. This is the key to your success. Spend some time thinking about what you could achieve if you didn't have to struggle with your shyness. If you can focus on what you could do, then the desire to achieve that will turn out to be stronger than the shyness that is holding you back. Keep the focus and the shyness will go away.

Action Is The Key To Long Term Success

When we are dealing with shyness, it can be all too easy to want to stay at home and not take on all of the risks associated with going out into the cruel world and giving a speech. Resist this urge and **make sure that you show up!** I realize that this can be tough to do, but once you make the effort to go, you'll be that much farther along in overcoming your shyness.

Finally, in order to successfully overcome your shyness you need to have a plan. The plan has to relate to why you are willing to get up and give speeches in the first place. This all has to be **leading to some goal that you want to achieve**. If you can identify that goal, then every step that you take in overcoming your shyness will be taking you one step close to realizing your plan.

What All Of This Means For You

Shyness is a fact of life for everyone. It can be overcome, but we need to take a number of different steps in order to accomplish this task and be able to share the benefits of public speaking with our audiences.

Right off the bat we need to develop a skill that we can be proud of. Using this skill, we can start to give speeches to friends and family members and then push our circle of audience members out to start to include strangers. The goal is to make our desire to speak stronger than our fear of speaking. We always have to keep in mind that no matter how much we fear it, we need to get up and show up **so that our next speech can become part of our overall plan**.

The wonderful thing about tacking your shyness is that **it can be overcome**. Once you've conquered it, it won't come back. Later on, you'll look back and be amazed at just how much your shyness was holding you back. Start to tackle it today!

Chapter 10

How Good Of A Speaker You Are Depends On How Well You See Yourself

Chapter 10: How Good Of A Speaker You Are Depends On How Well You See Yourself

Every speaker wants the same thing – **to become a better speaker**. The challenge that we all have is that although we understand the importance of public speaking, often we don't know what we need to change in order to become better. The secret to solving this problem is to take the time to see ourselves the way that our audience does.

How To Evaluate Your Next Speech

Imagine for a moment that **you are a professional sports star**. You are only going to remain a part of the game if you keep getting better and better. How are you going to go about doing that? Today's modern athletes get better at what they do by taking the time to study how they did it last time. They identify where they need to improve, work on their skills, and then move their game up to the next level.

As public speakers, we need to be doing the same thing. You'll never get better if you don't take the time to **study how your last speech went**. You are at a fundamental disadvantage every time you give a speech – you can't watch yourself while you are giving the speech. This means that you're going to have to come up with a different plan.

The simplest way to evaluate your performance during a speech is to pause while you are delivering the speech and evaluate your audience's reaction to the speech. Do they seem to be interested or are they "not with you"? Do this evaluation a few times throughout your speech in order to **see if your audience is staying with you**.

An even better way to get an evaluation of your next speech is to **either videotape yourself or plant some evaluators in the**

audience. Either way you'll get straight and honest feedback on how you did. Each time that you do this, you'll get a little bit better and you'll be able to improve your game the next time you give a speech.

Getting Off Autopilot

There was a diet that was popular a few years ago that was all about getting your body to be in "the zone". The thinking is that once you got there, **the extra pounds would just slide off of you**. This might be a great way to lose weight, but it's a lousy way to give a speech.

All too often speakers can develop **patterns of giving a speech** that will distract from the speech itself. These patterns can include things that you do with your hands such as touching your hair or fixing your clothes while speaking. It may have something to do with the words that you say – some phrase that you repeat over and over again.

We do these things on autopilot and we are generally not aware that we're doing them. In order to shut off our autopilot, we need to have someone watch our next speech and make notes about the things that we seem to be doing over and over again without being aware that we are doing them. After the speech is over, we need to have a talk with this person, learn from what they tell us, and then when we practice for our next speech we need to work to turn our personal autopilot off.

Becoming Better

Every speaker reaches a certain point in their speaking path where they may start to think that they are **"good enough"**. This is when they believe that they are a better speaker than a lot of other people and they may find it hard to keep improving.

We need to understand that **we always need to be working to become better**. Yes, change in any form is difficult and uncomfortable. Change is not something that will happen overnight. In fact, it might not happen by the time that you are called on to give your next speech. The good news is that change does not have to happen all at once – it can happen little-by-little. Just as long as we are getting better every time that we give a speech, we will be making the progress that we need to be making.

It is by changing that we can find ways **to better serve our audiences**. The reason that we can screw up the courage to get up in front of that audience and deliver a speech in the first place is because we believe that by doing so we can, in some little way, change the world. In order to make this happen, we need to always be looking for ways to become better at giving powerful speeches.

What All Of This Means For You

The speaker that you were yesterday is not as good as the speaker that you are today. The speaker that you will be tomorrow **will be better than the speaker that you are today**. The key is to find out just exactly how to become better.

In order to improve our speaking abilities, we need to first find a way to **evaluate our performance during our last speech**. Next we need to identify and stop doing those actions that we do on autopilot during a speech. Finally, once we know how to become better, we need to commit ourselves to becoming better.

One of the benefits of public speaking is that it truly is possible to **become a better speaker with each and every speech that we give**. However, this isn't going to happen by magic. Instead, what need to occur is that we need to learn how to evaluate our last speaking performance and then we need to use what we've learned to become better. It's possible, now get to it!

Chapter 11

New Techniques For Dealing With Every Speaker's Biggest Fear: Stage Fright

Chapter 11: New Techniques For Dealing With Every Speaker's Biggest Fear: Stage Fright

We'd all like to become better public speakers. However, that's simply not going to happen if we are too afraid to get up there and give our speech. Even if we can get on stage, no matter how good our audience's listening skills are, we may be constantly battling our fears and it's going to take away from the speech that we give. **How can a speaker overcome stage fright?**

It Turns Out That Stage Fright Is Normal

I know that the first time that I encountered stage fright I was both **surprised and alarmed**. What was going on? I had never felt so afraid about doing something that I knew that I had to do. Presentation tips were not going to solve this problem for me.

It turns out that stage fright is actually **a very natural human emotion**. What's going on is that we are reaching way back in time and drawing on the very skills that kept our caveman ancestors alive: fight or flight.

I think that we can all agree that giving a speech to an audience of 1 – 1,000 people can be classified as **a threating situation**. When faced with a situation like this, you will become fearful and that fight or flight mechanism will kick in and you'll be dealing with a case of stage fright. However, due to the importance of public speaking, you are going to have to find a way to get over it.

What you need to do is to accept how you feel. **Don't fight it**. It is, after all, a very natural reaction to the situation that you find yourself in. Instead of focusing on how you are currently feeling, shift your focus to the task at hand. This won't make your stage fright go away, but will make it easier to deal with.

Channel Your Creativity

When you know that you'll be dealing with stage fright, you often start to **get creative**. This is not always a good thing.

Speakers have been known to do a wide variety of **different physical activities** in order to attempt to deal with the stage fright that they are experiencing. This can include making their legs rigid or tightening up their chest.

It turns out that these are exactly the wrong things to be doing. They are going to have an obvious impact on how you deliver your speech – **you are going to sound different** because of all of the things that you are trying to do at the same time.

Instead of trying any of these tricks that are just going to have a negative impact on the speech that you end up giving, instead **channel your creativity**. Stage fright generates energy. Nervous energy that is. Harness this energy and use it to create a better speech. Pour yourself into creating a speech that uses all of your energy and create a speech that is going to use that energy to both grab and hold your audience's attention.

What All Of This Means For You

Stage fright is a natural part of life for public speakers – get over it. Going all the way back to when cavemen were walking around, we've always had a fight or flight reaction to threating situations.

We should not try to fight our stage fright sensations. They truly are **a natural part of who we are**. Accept how you are feeling and move on and don't let it impact the benefits of public speaking that you are delivering. Take the nervous energy that stage fright causes and channel it into creating an even better speech for your audience.

There is an old saying that if you don't feel fear, then you're not alive. In thinking about your next speaking opportunity I suspect that you are very much aware that you are alive – **that's some real fear that you are feeling!** Stop trying to fight it and use it to make better speeches and you'll have found a way to conquer your stage fright!

Chapter 12

Your Speech Is Not Over When You Are Done Talking

Chapter 12: Your Speech Is Not Over When You Are Done Talking

When is a speech really over? Is it when the last word has passed your lips? Is it when you step down off of the stage? It turns out that neither of these answers is correct. Your next speech won't be over **until your audience tells you that it's over**.

Why What Happens After A Speech Is So Very Important

I don't know about you, but after I get done speaking I'm drained. I just want to get off the stage, sit down, and take a load off. However, it turns out that this is never what my audience wants me to do. Instead, they view the completion of my speech as **the opening act in the next part of my presentation**. This all has to do with the importance of public speaking.

My audience has **a number of different needs**. They want to meet me. They want to shake my hand. They want to have a photograph taken with me. The list goes on.

What I always have to remind myself is that interacting with my audience after my speech is over is a key part of the speech. One can think of this as being a kind of **post speech performance**. My audience expects me to be the same person after my speech as I appeared to be when I was giving my speech.

Three Ways To Accept Praise Gracefully

One of the most difficult things that I've had to learn how to do after a speech was over is to accept praise from my audience. I don't get a lot of praise every day and so this is not something that I'm used to. The first thing that I struggle with is when people complement me and tell me that my speech was fantastic. My gut reaction is **to disagree with them**. I've learned that it is much better to not contradict what my audience is telling me and instead I just go along with it.

With a crush of audience members swarming you after you give a speech, they all want to tell you something. You're not going to have enough time to have a long drawn-out talk with each of them. I've discovered that you need to **keep your interaction with each member of your audience short and simple**. What I've discovered works best is a simple "thank you".

Finally, when you are responding to the praise that your audience is showing to you, **you need to be sincere in your responses**. Your audience will be able to tell if you don't mean what you are saying and that will make you appear to be very conceited. Take the time to acknowledge each person who showers you with praise and thank them for their kind words.

What All Of This Means For You

The next time that you give a speech you need to realize that just because you've stopped talking, **your speech is not over**. You need to think of every time that you give a speech as being an event and that event is not over until your audience tells you that it's over. One of the benefits of public speaking for your audience is what happens after you are done giving your speech.

What this means for you is that **you need to take the time to interact with your audience after you speech is done**. This is going to be critical in establishing how your audience views you – will they ever want to hear another speech from you? Use one of the 3 ways that we discussed to gracefully accept praise from your audience.

One way to think about your next speech is that **it's really just the beginning of your interaction with your audience**. The actual opportunity to interact and connect with your audience won't be over until they tell you that it's over. Make sure that you take the time to have a positive interaction with your audience after you complete your speech and your audience will leave with a positive impression of both you and your speech.

It's from the forge of failure that the steel of success is formed.

Hard Work Does Not Guarantee Success, But Success Does Not Happen Without Hard Work.

— Dr. Jim Anderson

Create Speeches That Motivate Your Audiences And Get Your Message Heard!

Dr. Jim Anderson is available to provide training and coaching on the topics that are the most important to people who have to speak in public: how can I create a speech that people want to hear and how can I deliver in a way that will allow me to connect with my audience and get my point across to them?

Dr. Anderson believes that in order to both learn and remember what he says, speakers need to laugh. Each one of his speeches is full of fun and humor so that what he says "sticks" with everyone.

Dr. Anderson's Public Speaking Training Includes:

1. How to plan your next speech: pick your purpose and understand your audience.
2. What's the best way to get PowerPoint and Keynote to work with you, not against you?
3. What do you need to do when you are presenting in order to truly connect with your audience?

Dr. Jim Anderson presents over 100 speeches per year. To invite Dr. Anderson to speak at your event, contact him at:

Phone: 813-418-6970 or
Email: jim@BlueElephantConsulting.com

Photo Credits:

Cover - Vic
https://www.flickr.com/photos/59632563@N04/

Chapter 1 - madamepsychosis
https://www.flickr.com/photos/belljar/

Chapter 2 - Insomnia Cured Here
https://www.flickr.com/photos/tom-margie/

Chapter 3 – Dr. Jim Anderson

Chapter 4 – 7263255
https://www.flickr.com/photos/7363531@N05/

Chapter 5 – Harmony
https://www.flickr.com/photos/fonticulus/

Chapter 6 - Michael K
https://www.flickr.com/photos/vasto/

Chapter 7 - Hans Splinter
https://www.flickr.com/photos/archeon/

Chapter 8 - Freddie Peña
https://www.flickr.com/photos/fixem/

Chapter 9 – spanaut
https://www.flickr.com/photos/cs___/

Chapter 10 - 0Four
https://www.flickr.com/photos/44456430@N04/

Chapter 11 - Andy Roberts
https://www.flickr.com/photos/aroberts/

Chapter 12 - Tom Gill
https://www.flickr.com/photos/lapstrake/

Other Books By The Author

Product Management

- How Product Managers Can Sell More Of Their Product: Tips & Techniques For Product Managers To Better Understand How To Sell Their Product

- How To Create A Successful Product That Customers Will Want: Techniques For Product Managers To Boost Product Sales And Increase Customer Satisfaction

- What Product Managers Need To Know About World-Class Product Development: How Product Managers Can Create Successful Products

- How Product Managers Can Learn To Understand Their Customers: Techniques For Product Managers To Better Understand What Their Customers Really Want

- Product Management Secrets: Techniques For Product Managers To Boost Product Sales And Increase Customer Satisfaction

- Product Development Lessons For Product Managers: How Product Managers Can Create Successful Products

- Customer Lessons For Product Managers: Techniques For Product Managers To Better Understand What Their Customers Really Want

- Product Failure Lessons For Product Managers: Examples Of Products That Have Failed For Product Managers To Learn From

- Communication Skills For Product Managers: The Communication Skills That Product Managers Need To Know How To Use In Order To Have A Successful Product

- How To Have A Successful Product Manager Career: The Things That You Need To Be Doing TODAY In Order To Have A Successful Product Manager Career

- Product Manager Product Success: How to keep your product on track and make it become a success

Public Speaking

- Delivering Excellence: How To Give Presentations That Make A Difference: Presentation techniques that will transform a speech into a memorable event

- Tools Speakers Need In Order To Give The Perfect Speech: What tools to use to create your next speech so that your message will be remembered forever!

- How To Create A Speech That Will Be Remembered

- Secrets To Organizing A Speech For Maximum Impact: How to put together a speech that will capture and hold your audience's attention

- How To Become A Better Speaker By Changing How You Speak: Change techniques that will transform a speech into a memorable event

- How To Give A Great Presentation: Presentation techniques that will transform a speech into a memorable event

- How To Rehearse In Order To Give The Perfect Speech: How to effectively rehearse your next speech to that your message be remembered forever!

- Secrets To Creating The Perfect Speech: How to create a speech that will make your message be remembered forever!

- Secrets To Organizing The Perfect Speech: How to organize the best speech of your life!

- Secrets To Planning The Perfect Speech: How to plan to give the best speech of your life

- How To Show What You Mean During A Presentation: How to use visual techniques to transform a speech into a memorable event

CIO Skills

- What CIOs Need To Know In Order To Successfully Manage An IT Department: Decision Making Skills That Every CIO Needs To Have In Order To Be Able To Make The Right Choices

- Becoming A Powerful And Effective Leader: Tips And Techniques That IT Managers Can Use In Order To Develop Leadership Skills

- CIO Secrets For Growing Innovation: Tips And Techniques For CIOs To Use In Order To Make

Innovation Happen In Their IT Department

- Your Success As A CIO Depends On How Well You Communicate: Tips And Techniques For CIOs To Use In Order To Become Better Communicators

- What CIOs Need To Know About Working With Partners: Techniques For CIOs To Use In Order To Be Able To Successfully Work With Partners

- Critical CIO Management Skills: Decision Making Skills That Every CIO Needs To Have In Order To Be Able To Make The Right Choices

- How CIOs Can Make Innovation Happen: Tips And Techniques For CIOs To Use In Order To Make Innovation Happen In Their IT Department

- CIO Communication Skills Secrets: Tips And Techniques For CIOs To Use In Order To Become Better Communicators

- Managing Your CIO Career: Steps That CIOs Have To Take In Order To Have A Long And Successful Career

- CIO Business Skills: How CIOs can work effectively with the rest of the company!

IT Manager Skills

- Save Yourself, Save Your Job – How To Manage Your IT Career: Secrets That IT Managers Can Use In Order To Have A Successful Career

- Growing Your CIO Career: How CIOs Can Work With The Entire Company In Order To Be Successful

- How IT Managers Can Make Innovation Happen: Tips And Techniques For IT Managers To Use In Order To Make Innovation Happen In Their Teams

- Staffing Skills IT Managers Must Have: Tips And Techniques That IT Managers Can Use In Order To Correctly Staff Their Teams

- Secrets Of Effective Leadership For IT Managers: Tips And Techniques That IT Managers Can Use In Order To Develop Leadership Skills

- IT Manager Career Secrets: Tips And Techniques That IT Managers Can Use In Order To Have A Successful Career

- IT Manager Budgeting Skills: How IT Managers Can Request, Manage, Use, And Track Their Funding

- Secrets Of Managing Budgets: What IT Managers Need To Know In Order To Understand How Their

Company Uses Money

Negotiating

- Use The Power Of Arguing To Win Your Next Negotiation: How To Develop The Skill Of Effective Arguing In A Negotiation In Order To Get The Best Possible Outcome

- Learn How To Signal In Your Next Negotiation: How To Develop The Skill Of Effective Signaling In A Negotiation In Order To Get The Best Possible Outcome

- Learn The Skill Of Exploring In A Negotiation: How To Develop The Skill Of Exploring What Is Possible In A Negotiation In Order To Reach The Best Possible Deal

- Learn How To Argue In Your Next Negotiation: How To Develop The Skill Of Effective Arguing In A Negotiation In Order To Get The Best Possible Outcome|

- How To Open Your Next Negotiation: How To Start A Negotiation In Order To Get The Best Possible Outcome

- Preparing For Your Next Negotiation: What You Need To Do BEFORE A Negotiation Starts In Order To Get The Best Possible Deal

- Learn How To Package Trades In Your Next Negotiation

- All Good Things Come To An End: How To Close A Negotiation - How To Develop The Skill Of Closing In Order To Get The Best Possible Outcome From A Negotiation

- Take No Prisoners In Your Next Negotiation: How To Start A Negotiation In Order To Get The Best Possible Outcome

Miscellaneous

- How To Heal A Broken Leg – Fast!: Understanding how to deal with a broken leg in order to start walking again quickly

- How Software Defined Networking (SDN) Is Going To Change Your World Forever: The Revolution In Network Design And How It Affects You

- The Power Of Virtualization: How It Affects Memory, Servers, and Storage: The Revolution In

Creating Virtual Devices And How It Affects You

- The Internet-Enabled Successful School District Superintendent: How To Use The Internet To Boost Parental Involvement In Your Schools

- Power Distribution Unit (PDU) Secrets: What Everyone Who Works In A Data Center Needs To Know!

- Making The Jump: How To Land Your Dream Job When You Get Out Of College!

- How To Use The Internet To Create Successful Students And Involved Parents

"Change techniques that will transform a speech into a memorable event

This book has been written with one goal in mind – to show you how you can present a powerful and effective speech. We're going to show you how to use the tools that every speaker has to deliver a great speech!

Let's Make Your Next Speech A Success!

What You'll Find Inside:

- **HOW SPEAKERS HANDLE THAT FEAR THING...**

- **GREAT SPEAKERS AREN'T AFRAID TO STUMBLE ON THE WAY TO THE TOP**

- **TOO SHY, SHY – HOW TO OVERCOME YOUR SHYNESS AND BECOME A PUBLIC SPEAKER**

- **YOUR SPEECH IS NOT OVER WHEN YOU ARE DONE TALKING**

Dr. Jim Anderson brings his 25 years of real-world experience to this book. He's delivered speeches at some of the world's largest firms as well as at many conferences. He's going to show you what you need to do in order to make your next speech a success!

www.ingramcontent.com/pod-product-compliance
Lightning Source LLC
Chambersburg PA
CBHW061200180526
45170CB00002B/894